60 NATURAL REMEDIES TO GUILT, ANXIETY, SLEEP LOSS & SADNESS

(2nd Edition)

How to Free Yourself from Guilt, Anxiety, Sleep Loss & Sadness through Nature

60 NATURAL REMEDIES TO GUILT, ANXIETY, SLEEP LOSS & SADNESS

(2nd Edition)

How to Free Yourself from Guilt, Anxiety, Sleep Loss & Sadness through Nature

DR. JOHN ZEDGENBROTH JOE, PHD

Theologian, Psychologist, Author, Asso. Professor and CEO

(University Of Arusha-Tanzania, Spicer College and Maharshi Dayanand University, India)

PhD Psychology (Maharshi Dayanand University, India)

Official Website: johnzedgenbrothjoe.weebly.com

Email: sharegodslove.withhischildren@gmail.com

Copyright © September 2014- **John Zedgenbroth Joe, PhD**

First Edition: 2014

Publisher: Create Space Publishing, USA

ISBN: 9781514132289

Second Edition: 2024

More about the Author

Dr. John Zedgenbroth Joe, PhD (Born John Mwaniki Njue) popularly in Asia known as Prime, is a New 21st Century young Theologian, Psychologist, Author, Poet, Researcher, Asso. Professor and CEO of The Zedgenbroth Foundation. He is known as the first and youngest Psychologist in the world ever known to discover HMQ and MC/MMC Testing (On Moral Intelligence and Mind Compatibility especially for every couple before their Marriage). He is also accredited to JFML Theory, Testhor Theory, Psychosexuation and Psychemoanalysis; a field in psychology related to Freud's Psychoanalysis. He has done research from many countries in the world and his classic and inspirational writings have touched and changed many lives of people in different countries. He is the author of the popular books "*The Secrets Of A Woman's Mind, Mental Health & Happiness,*" "*Woman's Mind Innermost Hidden Secrets,*" "*Women's Precious Fountain Of Well-being and Happiness,*"

4

"Your Mind Opener,""60 Natural Remedies to Guilt, Anxiety, Sleep Loss & Sadness,""63 Natural Remedies to Stress and Depression with A-Z of Happiness," "How It All Just Began," "Life Long Pictures," and "Life Long Pictures 2 (Journeys to the Planet of Darkness) the books which have transformed many people around the globe. He builds new dreams and work to achieve them by the hand of God. He is much motivated by a one verse from the bible in the book of Philippians 4:13 "I can do all things through Christ who strengthens me." His works will be remembered by all generations forever.

Author Review

The bestselling author of "63 Natural Remedies to Stress and Depression with A-Z Of Happiness" And "How It All Just Began"

General Editorial Review

Dr. John Zedgenbroth Joe has explored the world and found that many people are suffering from guilt for their past life mistakes. Others are going through worries in life, which make their current lives a misery. Due to many burdens in life, he finds some are not even able to sleep or lack enough sleep. Some are sad in life, they live a life of regretting, pains, discomforts. Nothing seems good in life.

You have tried all ways in life, but not even one is working. But even though life seems like a furnace, and not even one thing seems to cool it, still there is one more special and unique way left Joe has identified and which can turn your life in to a laughter and joy and according to him this is "The NATURE."

Book Review

A classic Dr. Joe's Bestselling book on how to utilize nature in conquering Guilt, Anxiety, Sleep loss and Sadness. Dr. Joe is a young psychologist who has gone into a deeper study and discovered that nature can be used as a psychological treatment of Guilt, Anxiety, Sleep Loss and Sadness. He uses beautiful terms like "Psycho hydrotherapy" meaning use of water as a natural therapy to treatment of psychological problems.

Very classic and unique book from a talented author.

Dedicated to:

Primarily to my beloved brother Cyrus Mugendi Njue (Joe) for being my trustworthy brother and friend in different aspects of life. Secondly dedicated to all my dear relatives and friends.

Guilt, anxiety, sleep loss and sadness are among the topper causes of major of human discomforts and hopeless life. In daily life I face a mass number of people suffering from guilt for their past life mistakes. Others are going through worries in life which make their current lives a misery. Due to many burdens in life, some are not even able to sleep or lack enough sleep. Some are sad in life, they live a life of regretting, pains, discomforts. Nothing seems good in life. You have tried all ways in life, but not even one is working. But even though life seems like a furnace and not even one thing seems to cool it, still there is one more special and unique way left which can turn your life in to a laughter and joy. Guess what is it?-----"The NATURE."

Nature provides us with a wonderful atmosphere to help us carry many burdens in life. This is practical volume of book which carries numerous natural remedies to guilt, anxiety, sleep loss and sadness. You will learn many causes of human discomforts like what causes guilt, worries, sleep loss, and sadness in daily life. Eventually, you are going to find in this book many many natural ways you can use to avoid them, free from them, conquer them and finally achieve an ultimate mental health naturally and free without any cost. The nature has the ability to bring many changes in your life, transforming you, reforming you and eventually gives you a resting place for all your burdens so that you can be free and happier in life. I believe that this book will finally or eventually give all human beings their minds and spirits a resting place and the atmosphere of ease feeling and beauty of special happiness. The things prescribed here are from day today life and they are practical and easy to do freely without any cost. Many have tried and they have achieved their complete mental health and ultimate happiness. Why don't you try today and achieve your well-being hence happier in life.

Dr. John Zedgenbroth Joe, PhD

Contents

CHAPTER 1

NATURE AND GUILT, ANXIETY, SLEEP LOSS & SADNESS

CHAPTER SUMMARY

Guilt, Anxiety, Sleep Loss and Sadness

The Beauty of the Nature

What involves the Nature?

What is 'Natural Remedies?'

Application of Remedies in this Book

Is there another main focus of Nature apart from Healing?

Why Did I write this book?

Other Secrets about Nature

GUILT, ANXIETY, SLEEP LOSS AND SADNESS

As I have said earlier, Guilt, anxiety, sleep loss and sadness are among the topper causes of major of human discomforts and hopeless life.

In daily life I face a mass number of people suffering from guilt for their past life mistakes. Others are going through worries in life, which make their lives a misery. Due to many burdens in life, some are not even able to sleep or lack enough sleep. Some are sad in life; they live a life of regretting, pains, discomforts and many more. Nothing seems good in life.

We are all living in a world of pain and dangers of unforeseen threats and failures. Guilt has become one of many people's troubles in life. It is true that we live in the world of calamities, mourning, anguish, devastation, hatred, guilt, infidelities, betrayal and death. Every day are troubles and tears from many many areas of life. Some are going through worries from:

- The family relations
- Work tensions
- Diseases

- Studies
- Death
- Poverty
- And many more.

Some are passing through hot paths of depressions and Sleep loss due to;

- Loss of loved ones
- Broken relationships
- Infidelity from their husband or wife
- Pornography
- Diseases
- Wars and disasters
- Lack of Employments
- And many more.

Others wish to end their lives due to every day troubles. But despite this, there is always a solution which has been existing around us. **NATURE.** Nature is natural in nature and a natural way to conquering many obstacles and devastation in life and eventually achieving a complete health including mental health.

Yes, we all can still achieve mental health and happiness. All men and women including children can prevent themselves from guilt, anxiety and sadness. We all can stand out and fight against pornography---the present day marriages major cause of sadness and marriages killer. Men and women can conquer worries and anxieties and live with bright hope of the future. We all can achieve ultimate happiness and never-ending joy of the heart and mind.

In many ways someone somewhere is asking;

- ❖ How can I be free from my past sins, mistakes, guilt and pain?
- ❖ Or how can I be free from my future worries and anxiety?
- ❖ Or how can I be happy again after losing my husband, boyfriend, dad, mother, sister, brother?
- ❖ How can I be happy again after being cheated by my husband or my partner?
- ❖ How can I be happy again after now I got divorced?

The question you must be asking now is; How can this be possible to attain happiness in this painful and restless world? It looks hard to achieve that right? But I want to tell you it is the easiest thing to do in this world. But how? **Through the nature**.

THE BEAUTY OF THE NATURE

I want to say that "Nature is Nurture." It is capable of nourishing and nurturing the creation. The creation here means all things which God created including the nature itself. The nature then is meant to ensure that living things which are part of creations are nurtured and nourished to ensure their facilitation of their well-being. And hence nature is meant to nurture human being, by protecting, securing, nourishing and preventing human from many dangers in life including diseases.

WHAT INVOLVES THE NATURE?

Nature involves all natural things like;

- ✓ Sun
- ✓ Moon
- ✓ Stars
- ✓ Sky

- ✓ Clouds
- ✓ Trees
- ✓ Rivers and water
- ✓ Fruits
- ✓ Vegetables
- ✓ Nuts
- ✓ Air
- ✓ Plants
- ✓ Flowers
- ✓ And many more.

The nature surrounds us and acts as our guards every day.

In addition, **human beings** are part of nature including,

- ➢ Songs
- ➢ Reading word of God,
- ➢ Animals
- ➢ Birds
- ➢ Grass
- ➢ Lakes,
- ➢ Oceans
- ➢ Beaches
- ➢ Seas
- ➢ Exercise
- ➢ Tour
- ➢ Mountain and climbing
- ➢ Swimming

➤ And many many more comprise the nature.

Hence, the word nature is quite broad enough to cover many God's created things.

WHAT IS 'NATURAL REMEDIES?'

Natural remedies are ways in which you can utilize the nature to benefit you in solving your problems. This benefit can be;

✓ Preventing against a disease
✓ Curing
✓ Healing
✓ Securing
✓ Nourishing
✓ Supplementing
✓ Counseling
✓ Directing
✓ Improving health and well-being
✓ And many more.

In most cases, when a word remedy is used, is meant to mean treatment of a disease. But as we have seen, remedy means more than treating.

APPLICATION OF REMEDIES IN THIS BOOK

This volume of book carries numerous natural remedies to help you prevent yourself from;

- ✓ Guilt
- ✓ Anxiety
- ✓ Sleep loss and
- ✓ Sadness.

In this book you will learn many causes of;

- Human discomforts
- Sadness
- Mental disturbances
- Guilt
- And many more things

causing all to spend their lives in pain of guilt, worries, in slavery, and hence unhappy in their lives and eventually you will see many many natural ways you can use to avoid them, free from them, conquer them and finally achieve an ultimate mental health naturally and free without any cost.

IS THERE ANOTHER MAIN FOCUS OF NATURE APART FROM HEALING?

There is more to have from nature apart from prevention and healing. The volume also moves on to explaining many ways we all can be **happier** in life. Through living a;

- ✓ Stress free
- ✓ Depression free
- ✓ Suicidal thoughts free
- ✓ Guilt free
- ✓ Anxiety free
- ✓ And many more.

We all can be able to achieve the ultimate freedom and eventually achieving the most **precious fountain of happiness** in all stages of our lives.

WHY DID I WRITE THIS BOOK?

I see every day people suffering from guilt, anxiety, and sadness. Others lack enough sleep or no sleep at all. They have tried much but they never find any help. But after applying nature in my life, I find very significant changes in my health and well-being and life and eventually I find lots of happiness in solving many problems through nature and I feel I should share my benefits with someone else. This book I wrote it to be all human kinds **'resting place** and a place they can **free** themselves from day today many dangers and threats of their lives. When dangers come in life someone can run into this book and find a resting place for his or her life troubles through applying easy to do natural keys to open the room for more happiness in his or her life.

Eventually, giving you the atmosphere of **ease feeling** and **beauty** of **special happiness and joy.** The things prescribed here are from day today life and they are easy to do freely without any cost.

Do them every day and you will find your life in lots of happiness and joy from people, nature and God.

Eventually, you find yourself asking, "How did I make it to all this never-ending precious river of happiness?"

I personally, wholeheartedly, thank God for everything in life specially creating the **NATURE.**

OTHER SECRETS ABOUT NATURE

This is practical volume of book which carries numerous natural remedies to guilt, anxiety, sleep loss and sadness. In this book you will learn many causes of human discomforts, like what causes guilt, worries, sleep loss, and sadness in daily life.

Eventually, you are going to find in this book many many natural ways you can use to;

- ✓ Avoid them
- ✓ Free from them
- ✓ Conquer them
- ✓ And finally achieve an ultimate mental health naturally and free without any cost.

The nature has the ability to bring many changes in your life;

- **Transforming** you
- **Reforming** you and eventually gives you
- **A resting** place for all your burdens so that you can be
- **Free** and **happier** in life.

CHAPTER 2

GUILT

CHAPTER SUMMARY

Sigmund Freud's Psychoanalysis of Guilt

How Can we Measure Guilt?

Measurements of Guilt

Defense Mechanisms to Guilt

1. Repression (Force Against) Mechanism
2. Projection (Throw out) Mechanism
3. Individual Harm (Personal harm) Mechanism
4. Denial (Refusal) Mechanism
5. Suppression (Voluntary Press Against) Mechanism

Reactions to Guilt

1. Reaction Formation (Opposite Behavior Practice)
2. Rationalisation (Logical Thinking)
3. Deep out (Confession)

Lack of guilt in people with psychopathy

What Is Psychopathy?

Sources and Causes of All Human Guilt

What Is Guilt?

How Do I Personally Understand About Guilt?

Dr. John Zedgenbroth Joe's Psychemoanalysis of Guilt

How Did Sigmund Freud Understand about Guilt?

In this chapter we will be looking at guilt specifically; what is it, what it is understood by professionals, how to measure it, what it involves etc. We then can start by asking ourselves; what is it?

WHAT IS GUILT?

Guilt is a mental and emotional response which occurs when a person believes or feels that he or she has gone astray in his or her own standards of conduct or has gone against an accepted code of ethics or morals. This is one of the disorders affecting many people today especially women.

It is a mental disturbance as well as emotional in which one experiences threatening conflicts or fights in him/her for having done something that one believes should not have done. The experience is a teaching by itself whereby one is supposed to change as soon as possible. Unless one changes his or her behavior accompanied by guilt, he or she might never be free from this feeling.

I also term guilt as an **'Inner Judge'**. This is because it judges one's morality and rewards it. If one is doing what is right, he or she is rewarded with a good and happy feeling. If on the other hand someone does the contrary and acts immorally, one is rewarded with bad, sad and threatening feeling which is the guilt. Guilt is a major topic in Psychology that requires deep learning and understanding.

HOW DO I PERSONALLY UNDERSTAND ABOUT GUILT?

Dr. John Zedgenbroth Joe's Psychemoanalysis of Guilt

Psychemoanalysis a word I employed in HEMO psychology, refers to a process of a close examination or analysis of one's mind in order to relate his/her morality to his/her health and mental wellbeing. During psychemoanalysis, a person experiencing guilt scores a lower HMQ. HMQ (Health Moral Quotient) is the relationship between your morality and your health and wellbeing. A person who is suffering from guilt means that her morality is low, that is she must have done wrong. Hence low morality leads to a low health especially mental health and in this case, guilt is an example of a low mental health. And hence results to a low HMQ.

On the other hand, high morality leads to high health and mental health. For example, a person who is very careful in his or her conducts maintains a high level of morality and as a result, will experience good feelings and happiness in his or her life. For example, if you give a gift to a poor person and he says 'thank you' for the act, you will feel good and happy, right? This means that high level of morality, leads to high level of good feelings and happiness and hence high HMQ.

HOW DID SIGMUND FREUD UNDERSTAND ABOUT GUILT?

Sigmund Freud's Psychoanalysis of Guilt

Sigmund Freud described this feeling as, a result of a struggle between the ego and the superego. Freud rejected the role of God as punisher in times of illness or a rewarder in time of wellness. According to him guilt is as a result of superego punishing the ego. In other words, it is a punishment of someone's, immorality. While trying to terminate one origin of guilt from patients, he described another. This was the unconscious force or conflict within the person which contributed to illness or problem.

According to Freud, the obstacle of an unconscious sense of guilt is seen as the most powerful of all obstacles in life. This sounds true, since guilt really pains. It may lead even to sleep loss in some people.

HOW CAN WE MEASURE GUILT?

Measurements of Guilt

In psychology guilt can be measured by using various questionnaires and case studies of a person. An example of psychological questionnaires for measuring guilty feeling is Dutch Guilt Measurement Instrument (DGMI) and Differential Emotions Scale (DES) and many others.

On the other hand, if you want to relate guilt with the level of health and mental well-being, you use HEMO or HMQ test. I.e. Health Moral Quotient Test. You can see and read more about HEMO/HMQ in my book; *"Your Mind Opener."*

DEFENSE MECHANISMS TO GUILT

There are many defense mechanisms associated with guilt feeling. Here I will discuss some of them especially the one which come in the first stages of guilt. Now let's try and see some of them.

1. Repression (Involuntary Force Against) Mechanism

Repression I can define it as automatic or involuntary rejection of the unconscious conflicts or guilt. It seems to come from two words **'re'** which means again and **'press'** which means force or against. In other words, repression is a way of continuous force against one's guilt. It is a kind of argument in nature which takes place between one's super ego and ego. It is like superego is saying to the ego "you have done wrong" but ego disagrees and tries to defend itself saying, "No am innocent." The true is that superego always has to punish ego wherever ego does wrong. This punishment is now called guilt. An ego may repress against his or her guilt but superego is always strong and powerful to punish one with guilt until one ask for forgiveness and turns away from that immorality and also begins a new life.

2. Projection (Throw out) Mechanism

To **'project'** means to throw out or taking off something from one area to another. In other words, a person who feels guilty and finds that repression is not helping, will start blaming other people. This example of projection is clearly seen in the first book of the bible, Genesis 3, where Adam projects his faults towards Eve and later Eve projects towards the Serpent.

The idea of blaming others is not a solution to free ones from guilt. The most important solution towards guilt is 'acceptance' instead of projection. Accepting you have done wrong and asking for forgiveness and refraining from that immoral act and immediately starting a new life is the best solution towards guilt.

36

3. Individual Harm (Personal harm) Mechanism

Now once one projects instead of accepting his or her mistakes, still will not escape the punishment from superego. He or she will keep on feeling guilt continuously. In some people the guilt may last in decades until one confesses, repents and asks for forgiveness. In this case some people may think of even harming or punishing themselves. Again, this is not the better solution. The ultimate solution to any kind of guilt is accepting that 'yes' you have done wrong and asking for forgiveness.

4. Denial (Refusal) Mechanism

This refers to refusal to accept that you did wrong thing. One may feel guilty but instead of accepting the wrong he/she did, refuses it. It is very bad defense mechanism but no matter how one refuses to accept the wrong thing, cannot change the fact that he/she did wrong. This defense mechanism is very common practice by people.

5. Suppression (Voluntary Press Against) Mechanism

Unlike repression that is automatic or unconscious way of forgetting the wrong thing one did, suppression is conscious or voluntary way of forgetting the wrong thing one did. He/she puts more effort to forget what he/she did in order to overcome guilt feeling.

All these five defense mechanisms are not ultimate ways to get away from guilt. The repression, projection, self-harming, denial and even suppression are committed by those people with a low **forward thinking intelligence (FTI)** a form of lacking to think of or considering future repercussions or negative effects of doing wrong.

REACTIONS TO GUILT

After people have tried to defend themselves against guilty feeling, they are then likely to continue defending themselves or start reacting towards the feeling especially after sometime. Reaction means the positive steps they take after feeling guilty. Here we will look at three ways they are likely to react over the guilt.

1. Reaction Formation (Opposite Behavior Practice)

Reaction formation refers to tying to practice a new behavior that does not promote guilt. For example, if someone is feeling guilty because of stealing, he/she may try to practice the opposite behavior by trying to go to teach people not to steal and that it's wrong to steal. He/she tries to cover the guilt feeling by trying an opposite behavior. He may also try donating things to poor people so as to try to relieve himself/herself. This reaction can be practical if someone repents his/her wrong doing and asks for forgiveness from the victim and God.

2. Rationalisation (Logical Thinking)

Rationalisation refers to thinking in a logical way towards the cause of the guilt. For example, if feeling guilty because of stealing, rational way is trying to think that the only way to stop feeling guilty is returning what he/she stole. A person instead of arguing with himself/herself, tries to reason logically that the cause of his/her guilt is the wrong thing he/she did. Some people in life use this reaction to fight against the guilty feeling though some people practice the opposite behaviors or continue with the defense mechanisms.

3. Deep out (Confession)

Deep out refers to analysing through what is causing you guilt and taking it out either through sharing or confession. Here some people go to Psychologists or mental health experts for help. There are also those who go to their fellow friends or relatives and speak out what is disturbing them. While there are some who go to pastors and share what they are going through, some choose to react by confessing what they did to the offended and some go further; they confess to God.

LACK OF GUILT IN PEOPLE WITH PSYCHOPATHY

What Is Psychopathy?

However, still there are people who don't feel guilty even when they are harming other people. These people are called

psychopathetic people or **commonly psychopaths.** For example, there are people who bomb a massive people and even keep on killing them and never feel guilty.

Psychopathetic people I also newly term them as **"agnoiaic"** people or **"willful blind"**. The word 'agnoiaic' I derive it from a Greek word 'agnoia' which means ignorant person. They are willful blind because they do whatever they wish including harming others but don't see the harm or they don't feel guilty, hence "willful blind."

This is what I termed as **'backward thinkers'** or also **'dwarf minded'** people with lack ability to carefully evaluate situations in a moral aspect and also lacking abilities to develop moral or emotional intelligence.

From my recent research conducted in India 45% of all women participated in my survey, were going through guilty feeling about their past lives.

SOURCES AND CAUSES OF ALL HUMAN GUILT

There are many sources and causes of human guilt (to both men and women). As the Freud says, guilt is as a result of **immorality.** As I have mentioned in my books and I keep on repeating again and again, so that everyone can comprehend deeply, my saying; "Disobedience is the root of all immoralities, while immorality is the root of all pain." The reason most of people do suffer from guilt is because they have allowed themselves to be led by the flesh instead of the spirit. As Paul says, in Galatians 5:16-17 (text taken from the bible) "So I say, walk by the Spirit, and you will not gratify the desires of the flesh. 17 For the flesh desires what is contrary to the Spirit, and the Spirit what is contrary to the flesh. They are in **conflict with each other**, so that you are not to do whatever you want." Please note the bold phrase above, conflict **with each other'**, which shows that guilt arises when one goes against the spirit. This means that disobedience to God and following the desires of the flesh is the root cause of guilt or inner conflict.

Hence according to the bible which is the basis of all morality the following are the sources and causes of guilt as listed by Apostle Paul in Galatians 5:19:

1. Sexual immorality

Sexual immoralities are immoralities associated with sex. As I have mentioned in my books, premarital sex, extramarital sex and commercial sex practice are what Paul calls here sexual immorality and those who practice this end up experiencing guilt, stress, depression and even anxiety.

2. Impurity and debauchery

Impurity is opposite of purity. Purity here means **inner spiritual purity.** Anything that can make you impure can lead you to guilt.

3. Idolatry and witchcraft

Idolatry refers to worshiping of idols. This can also be a root cause of guilt especially when after you come to realize the true God. Coming to realize that you have been an atheist all this while or have been worshiping images or idols but there is a true God can cause some one guilt. But discovering the true God results in relieving you from all guilt, fear and anxiety.

4. Hatred

Hating someone especially without any reason can lead to guilt. Even when someone has done you wrong still hating him/her isn't the right thing. Even this can lead to guilt when you come to the light and see no good reason for hating him/her all that time.

5. Discord

When you disagree with others, after sometime you may feel guilty. You may start looking at the disagreement you made and see it was not glorifying God and eventually you may end up feeling guilty.

6. Jealousy

Feeling jealous of others can harm you and feel guilty afterwards.

7. Selfish ambition

Being selfish like when someone asks you for help and denies him or her the help, after sometime you may end up feeling guilty.

8. Dissensions

This is related to disagreement too and can also lead to guilt. Conflicting with other people which can lead to even quarrels, disunity, fight etc.

9. Factions

Factions can also lead to guilt feeling especially which lead to break up of united people to small groups or dissenting.

10. Envy

This is related to jealousy and can lead to a great guilt feeling. Envy is whereby someone doesn't feel happy when someone else is blessed by God. He/she feels bad for the other one's blessings or good things happening to him/her. Envy is great a sin before God. Instead of envy it is better to pray to God to bless you too.

11. Drunkenness

When you may drink alcohol and you come to realize you were drunk but you are not used to do that, or someone convinced you to drink but after drinking you come to your senses and realize that you went against your morals, you may feel guilty.

12 Orgies

Orgies refer to parties which involve drinking and sex. When you do this after you come to your senses, you may end up feeling guilty.

And the like

And the like means there are many more things that can cause someone guilt or other practices that are also considered sinful and can make people feel guilty. These could be:

- Theft
- Robbery
- Murder
- Rape
- Abortion
- Pride

- Watching pornography
- Cheating or lying
- Smoking
- Lack of respect to parents or elders
- Drugs abuse

And many more.

Paul adds and says, "I warn you, as I did before, that those who live like this will not inherit the kingdom of God."

This means that in addition to guilt suffering, those who practice such kind of things will never enter into the kingdom of God. And in the case of agnoiaic or psychopathy, they become ignorant now in what they do but their reward is awaiting them which is eternal fire. Hence disobedience to God is the root of all immorality, while immorality is the root of all pains and in this case guilt.

CHAPTER 3

10 NATURAL REMEDIES AND PSYCHOTHERAPIES TO GUILT

CHAPTER SUMMARY

10 Most Effective Natural Remedies to Relieve All Human from Guilt

A. 5 Psychological Psychotherapies and Natural Remedies
   Self-Examination
   Acceptance
   Action and Open Up
   Self-Forgiveness
   Synepial Learning

B. 5 Spiritual Psychotherapies and Remedies
   Spiritual Psychotherapy
   Others Forgiveness
   Self-Clearance
   Self-Rewarding
   New Lifestyle

In this chapter we will be looking at the natural remedies and psychotherapies which can be used to relieve all human (men and women) from guilty feeling.

10 MOST EFFECTIVE NATURAL REMEDIES TO RELIEVE ALL HUMAN FROM GUILT

Let me say that guilt is both **spiritual** disorder as well as **psychological** disorder. But both are related with each other. This means that one may feel guilty because has done an immoral thing (spiritual) hence starts suffering from guilt (psychological). This is what I termed in my new field in psychology, ' HEMO' Psychology which means that there is a close relationship between one's morality (MO) and his or her health (HE), hence HEMO psychology. For example, if one steals or rapes (immoralities) may suffer from guilt (poor health/mental well-being). But one who is moral may not suffer from guilt. Hence low morality leads to low health and mental well-being. Hence, I termed HEMO psychology or Health Moral Psychology.

50

Hence, in that case I will divide these natural remedies into two; 5 Psychological Psychotherapies and natural remedies and the last 5 Spiritual Psychotherapies and natural Remedies to guilt.

A. 5 PSYCHOLOGICAL PSYCHOTHERAPIES AND NATURAL REMEDIES

Self-Examination

1. Examine yourself carefully Why you Feel Guilty

When feeling guilt, the first thing or question you should ask yourself is, "Why am I feeling guilty?" This question is quite crucial and it will definitely take your mind back towards your past experience. Try and analyze carefully what you did and hold the incidence now in your hands, in your present.

Acceptance

2. Accept that you did wrong

After analyzing your past carefully, and holding that past in your hands at present, the next thing to do is to accept 'yes' I did wrong. "Yes, I wronged him/her," "yes, I wronged myself." Accepting reduces the pain of guilt over 50%. But repressing and projecting lead to self-harming. Acceptance here of what you are holding presently in your hands (mind) will lead to the next remedy 3.

3. Think of discussing the issue with the victim

Remember the victim can be either;

- Another person or living thing
- Yourself
- God

Discussing the issue with the victim seems to be the hardest remedy to guilt because some people might not feel confident to try and face the victim. For example, if you stole, you may find it hard to tell the person whom you stole from. In this case, you may ask **someone to help you to face the victim.** Or if finding it hard you may prefer just taking what you stole and going secretly and leave it in that person's home. In some cases, and to make it better you may write a letter without indicating your name but may be including your email address, indicating your confession to that person and asking for forgiveness. This letter is included together with what you stole.

Eventually, the victim will be surprised by the act and may contact you through that email address you provided saying thank you and has forgiven you. This is what I called **'moral intelligence'** because it shows how you are intelligent concerning your morality. However, a person who represses and projects as well as psychopathetic person lacks moral intelligence.

Now, in the case where you wronged yourself e.g. Abortion, alcoholism, smoking, drug abuse etc. or wronged God e.g. Idol worship, you may use the same remedy as well. Facing yourself is not harder as facing other victims. It's is very easy. Facing God is also very easy than facing other victims. After this remedy you need to move to the next remedy 4.

4. Apologize to yourself

After obtaining an apology from the victim, now just apologize to yourself. "I forgive myself just as am forgiven." This gives you a better feeling knowing that you are forgiven from the other side as well as your own side. Also, if you wronged yourself, this is the time to forgive yourself.

Synepial Learning

5. Get a lesson from the incidence and move forward newly

Synepial Learning is a learning I initiated in my book *"Woman's Mind Innermost Hidden Secrets"* as the second step to Psychemotherapy.

Synepial comes from Greek word 'synepeies' which means consequences. Synepial learning means that one learns after he/she foresees or encounters the negative consequences of his behavior. Synepial learning in this 5th remedy refers to **learning after the consequences of guilt** (e.g. bad mood, pain, stress, depression etc.). During (synepial learning) this second stage of psychemotherapy a client should know or be told his **General and Specific BE moral characteristic type** (read about BE moral characteristic in FML theory in my book *"Woman's Mind Innermost Hidden Secrets"*). A person sees and learns the consequences of his immoral life. He must learn that it's better to change before negative consequences of an immorality/bad behavior occur than changing after the consequences. For example, it is better to change before one catch Lung Cancer than after catching Lung Cancer, it is better to change before one catch STDs in sexual immorality than after one catch STDs etc.

After synepial learning (in psychemotherapy), the psychemotherapist can train the patient how to stop the specific or general immoral behavior like smoking, alcoholism, drugs abuse etc. through what I termed as **Subdoktrina learning** or simply SUBSTITUTION LEARNING in my book *"Woman's Mind Innermost Hidden Secrets"*.

After you have apologized to yourself in the remedy 4, the first thing you need to ask yourself is, "What lesson can I find behind this scene?" The fact is that every guilt is a reminder that we have not learnt from our past. Hence, when we apologize to the victims as well as to ourselves, we should then learn from our past mistakes and we avoid doing the same again. In other words, we acquire **moral intelligence or emotional intelligence.**

B. 5 SPIRITUAL PSYCHOTHERAPIES AND REMEDIES

Spiritual Psychotherapy

6. (1) Spiritual therapy

Spiritual therapy is the ultimate solution and remedy to guilty. I, as both a psychologist and theologian, have come to discover the power of spiritual psychotherapy after applying it to many guilty feeling patients. The spiritual psychotherapy requires the offender to renew his life with the offended and with God through confession.

King David is an example of a person in the bible who applied spiritual psychotherapy to relieve himself from pain. After David committing some of the causes of guilt I listed in the previous chapter; murder and adultery, (2 Samuel 11), in Psalms 51 realized it's only God who could make him feel relieved from guilt and experience joy and happiness in his life. He says in 51:1 (text taken from the bible) "Have mercy upon me, O God, according to thy loving-kindness: according unto the multitude of thy tender mercies blot out my transgressions. 2 Wash me thoroughly from mine iniquity, and cleanse me from my sin. 3 for I acknowledge my transgressions: and my sin is ever before me. 4 Against thee, thee only, have I sinned, and done this evil in thy sight: that thou mightiest be justified when thou speakest, and be clear when thou judgest...

7 Purge me with hyssop, and I shall be clean: wash me, and I shall be whiter than snow. 8 Make me to hear joy and gladness; that the bones which thou hast broken may rejoice. 9 Hide thy face from my sins, and blot out all mine iniquities. 10 Create in me a clean heart, O God; and renew a right spirit within me. 11 Cast me not away from thy presence; and take

not thy holy spirit from me. 12 Restore unto me the joy of thy salvation; and uphold me with thy free spirit. 13 Then will I teach transgressors thy ways; and sinners shall be converted unto thee. 14 Deliver me from **bloodguiltiness**, O God, thou God of my salvation: and my tongue shall sing aloud of thy righteousness."

Please note verse 14 "Deliver me from **bloodguiltiness**' O God..." which shows that David realized that only God would wash him fully and thoroughly from the guilt he was feeling.

Renewing your relationship with God and stopping the former wrong ways is the most ultimate natural remedy to guilt.

Others Forgiveness

7. (2) Seek Forgiveness from the Offended Person

Now this remedy has a connection with the psychological remedy 3 only that in the psychological remedy 3 one just thinks of discussing the issue with the victim and apologizing but in many cases, one benefits only psychologically and to some people the guilt may not be fully washed away. And hence this spiritual remedy is quite effective.

Renewing your relationship with God includes asking for forgiveness from the person you offended. God always require us to settle our faults with people before we ask for forgiveness from Him. Matthew 5:23 and 24, (Text from the bible) "Therefore if thou bring thy gift to the altar, and there rememberest that thy brother hath ought against thee, leave there thy gift before the altar, and go thy way; **first be reconciled** to thy brother, and then come and offer thy gift." This is only in the case where you feel guilty for doing wrong against other people. But regardless of clearing your fault or guilt with other people, you need to consult God for final cleansing and will reward you with amazing joy of relief and feel happy in life.

Self-Clearance

8. (3) Forgive Yourself

Forgiving yourself is the next thing in line. After the offended has forgiven you as well as God, you need now forgive yourself. Say that you are forgiven and you have never done anything wrong. God has forgiven you. The environment has forgiven you. Hence forgive yourself and be happy.

Self-Rewarding

9. (4) Go for a Self-Reinforcement or Self Rewarding

Self-reinforcement is a process whereby individuals control their own behaviors by rewarding themselves when a certain standard of performance has been attained. This is simply called rewarding. The method is psychological in nature but it can be applied as a spiritual natural remedy from guilt. Once you feel relieved the next thing is to reward yourself with a beautiful gift to make you feel as if you never did anything wrong. You may also say you want to self-reward yourself by going to church the next worship day and be the first in the church to arrive or buying for you a new bible. This is one way of allowing yourself to be free from the past wrong experiences.

10. (5) Adapting A New Lifestyle in Life

In addition, after you are relieved and happy in life, please adapt a new lifestyle from there. A lifestyle which avoids guilt and promotes happiness is described by the apostle Paul in the bible in Galatians 5:22 (text from the bible) "But the fruit of the Spirit is:

- -Love
- -Joy
- -Peace
- -Forbearance
- -Kindness
- -Goodness
- -Faithfulness
- -Gentleness
- -Self-control.

Against such things there is no law. 24 Those who belong to Christ Jesus have crucified the flesh with its passions and desires. 25 Since we live by the Spirit, let us keep in step with the Spirit."

This will shield you with the everlasting happiness and keep you away from guilt day and night for every day joy.

CHAPTER 4

ANXIETY

CHAPTER SUMMARY

What Is Anxiety?

4 Main Keys to help Differentiating Anxiety from Fear/Phobia (TLDL)

Who is at a higher Risk?
    Women at High Risk of Anxiety

Types of Anxiety and Fears/ Phobias

Point To Note

Risk Factors Associated with Anxiety and Phobias

How Can I Know Am Anxious?
    Symptoms and Signs of Anxiety

Diagnoses And Prevention

In this chapter we are going to look at the anxiety as well as phobias or fears. We will start by knowing what is anxiety and how is different to fear. Also, there are many types of anxiety and phobias in which we can look at some of them.

WHAT IS ANXIETY?

Anxiety is an unpleasant or sadness state of mind which occurs when one is expecting negative stimulus or happening to appear in his or her life in the future. It comes as a result of anticipating the future or going ahead of our life. When we think of "what if...?" This question is anxiety generative question because if one does not get a clear answer which is certain, he or she may feel worried. This is now anxiety. I may also term as, **'anticipatory disorder'** because it is a disorder which arises as a result of anticipating the future uncertainty. Anxiety just as stress and depression, is another mental as well as emotional disorder in nature and is composed of many types as we will be seeing in this chapter. It also has physical symptoms.

Anxiety sometimes is confused with fear. The simple difference between fear and anxiety is that, fear is a mental, emotional and physical response towards the **present** stimulus while anxiety is a mental, emotional and physical response towards future uncertain stimulus. For example, one may see a lion and may start shaking and crying. This is fear (phobia) because the stimulus is present. On the other hand, one may have similar responses of shaking and crying because exam is next week or a disease test results are coming out few minutes after now. This is now anxiety. Hence both have similar or related responses but the stimulus time is different.

4 MAIN KEYS TO HELP DIFFERENTIATING ANXIETY FROM FEAR/PHOBIA (TLDL)

T-Time

L-Length

D-Distance

L-Location

1. The Time

Usually, fear/phobia is associated with the present seen threat or stimulus, while anxiety is associated with future unforeseen threats.

2. The Length of mental or emotional response

Usually, the length of mental or emotional response of fear is shorter than that of anxiety. For example, you may shake shortly because of seeing a lion but after running away, you stop shaking immediately (fear). But you will shake more and for a long time until you see your exam results tomorrow (anxiety).

3. The Distance between the stimulus and response

Usually, the distance between the stimulus and the response is shorter in fear than in anxiety. For example, the distance between the seen lion and shaking (fear), is shorter than the distance between the disease test results you are waiting for and shaking or distance between shaking now and uncertain exam results tomorrow (anxiety).

4. The Location Of the threat or stimulus

Normally, the location of the threat in fear is seen but the location of the threat of anxiety is not yet seen.

WHO IS AT A HIGHER RISK?

Women at High Risk of Anxiety

As have indicated in some of my books about the differences of woman's mind to man's, the **anterior cingulate cortex**, is involved in making options, and is involved in anxiety. The part is larger in women than in men which makes it possible that most of women are more anxious than men.

In our daily life, if you look at it deeply, women seem to be more worried in nature than men. A small thing like remembering a certain negative thing in the past may lead to a woman even anticipating anxiety in the future.

Research demonstrates that anxiety is about four times more common in women than men. This means that it is very easily to find a woman who is much worried than finding a man with same disorder.

TYPES OF ANXIETY AND FEARS/ PHOBIAS

There many types of anxiety and fears (phobias). I will list a few of them. The disorder may exist in many ways like;

1. Obsessive Compulsive Disorder (OCD)

Obsessive Compulsive Disorder (OCD) is a type of anxiety which is characterized or involves a person worrying due to continuous disturbance of thoughts (obsession) and this continuous disturbance leads to someone doing things in a repetitive way (compulsion) as someone tries to obey his obsessions. For example, you may find someone washing his hands again and again.

2. Social Phobias (SP)

Social Phobias (SP) [not to be confused with specific phobias also SP in no. 4] are types of fears characterized by avoidance of public or social gatherings e.g., fear to speak in public.

People with Social phobias may show signs like, blushing of face, sweating, shaking, nausea, avoiding use of public things like toilets etc.

3. Post-Traumatic Stress Disorder (PTSD)

Post-Traumatic Stress Disorder (PTSD) is a type of anxiety which arises after one has gone through a certain negative incidence (trauma) like sexual abuse, accidents, a disease, surgery etc. and starts anticipating the future outcomes of the present trauma. This disorder involves; first **trauma**, followed by **stress** over the trauma, which accumulates and lead to the disorder (Post Post-Traumatic Stress Disorder). If not diagnosed on time may lead to depression.

4. Specific Phobias (SP)

Specific Phobias are types of phobias or fears which are caused by specific stimuli. For example, one sees a lion (stimulus) and starts shaking (response). This is a type of specific phobia since is caused by a specific stimulus (lion).

There are usually 5 types of specific phobias;

> ➤ Phobias caused by **Animals** e.g., fear of dogs

- ➢ Phobias caused by **Natural Environments** e.g., fear of height or climbing trees
- ➢ Phobias as a result of **specific situations** e.g., being alone in your room
- ➢ Phobias of **blood and injections** e.g., fear of blood, injections etc.
- ➢ **Other specific phobias** which are not listed either in any of the first four.

5. Existential Anxiety (EA)

Existential Anxiety (EA) is a type of anxiety which comes as result of existence. For example, there are those people who are worried of death. This is a type of existential anxiety. Knowing that you may die soon as a result of a chronic disease may trigger existential anxiety.

Other causes of existential anxiety can be like isolation and when finding no meaning in life. If you don't find the reason to live may cause this type of anxiety. Failures in life can be a cause also.

6. Panic Disorder (PD)

Panic Disorder (PD) results when something unexpected appears and leads to confusion of mind without knowing what else to do. For example, assume you are walking on a road, and a car appears in front of you abruptly, what may happen? You may stay in one place and wonder whether to keep on walking, just stand, or run. This is a panic and unless one has a **faster decision-making** process **(FDM)** in the **frontal lobe**, may even faint or fall down (collapse). FDM is a decision-making process which is initiated by frontal lobe of brain and may or may not be found with people with very superior IQ (Genius) e.g., IQ of 140. FDM people reason so fast and make decisions so quickly. For example, in a plane; a pilot may announce that no enough fuel for the plane to land even urgently. FDM person may not panic but may take or ask for a parachute and immediately when others are panicked FDM is out of plane.

7. Separation Anxiety Disorder (SAD)

Separation Anxiety Disorder (SAD) is a type of anxiety resulting from separation especially physically. It is common in children. A child may refuse to even go to school because doesn't want to separate with his/her mother/father or may even refuse to sleep away from home. This can be diagnosed as SAD depending with a continuous observation of the same behavior by the parents for quite some time. Diagnostic and Statics Manual (DSM IV) can be a very useful tool to help in diagnosing this disorder.

8. Generalized Anxiety Disorder (GAD)

Generalized Anxiety Disorder (GAD) refers to an anxiety which is not specific in nature. This means that the anxiety is not named after a certain specific cause. It cannot be grouped as in any of the previous 7 anxiety and phobias disorders. For example, PTSD is caused by Traumas, SAD as a result of separations, but GAD is not specific in nature. One may be worried of anything in life.

POINT TO NOTE

It is very important to note that, in most cases, these types of anxiety and phobia are caused by irrational **or cognitive distortions** in a mind of a person. Irrational means you can't have **logical evidence of that.** For example, you have a cancer, then get worried that you are going to die. WHO SAID

73

THAT YOU ARE GOING TO DIE? I write it in capital letter because it's rational or logical question.

WHERE IS THE EVIDENCE THAT THAT CANCER WILL NOT GET CURED? Even though someone died of cancer, that does not mean you will die. People are different and what may lead to death in this person, might not in another. This means that most of these disorders are avoidable in nature. How? **Through tuning and challenging our thinking.**

RISK FACTORS ASSOCIATED WITH ANXIETY AND PHOBIAS

The following risk factors are or might be associated with many types of anxiety and phobias;

Biological Causes
- Brain damage
- Accidents
- Etc.

Diseases

Diseases like;

74

- Measles
- Whooping cough
- Hydrocephalus
- etc.

Genetics

- Down syndrome

- Problem with genes

Immature birth of a person

- When a child is born immature, may lead to developing anxiety disorders or phobias.

Lack of Oxygen

- Lack of oxygen or enough oxygen at birth can also lead to anxiety or phobia later in life.

Alcohol Drinking

- Drinking alcohol by a pregnant woman can cause a child to be born to have anxiety or phobia later in life.

Neurotransmitters

- Dopamine
- Serotonin
- Norepinephrine

Cognitive Distortions
- Irrational thinking
- Unreasonable thinking
- Poor perception

Behavioral causes
- Previous experiences with a certain stimulus e.g. I fear today because that same dog chased me last time. I am having social phobia today because people embarrassment last time.
I am anxious to die because my neighbor died of the same disease.

Psychodynamic causes
- Inferiority complex
- Internal conflicts within a person

Existential factors
- Death
- Poverty
- Isolation
- Meaninglessness in life

HOW CAN I KNOW AM ANXIOUS?

Symptoms and Signs of Anxiety

Anxiety is both **mental** as well as **emotional** (includes physical) response towards seen (for phobias or fears) or unforeseen future stimulus and a threat. We will look at mental, emotional, physical and behavioral symptoms associated with anxiety and phobias:

1. Mental and Cognitive Symptoms

The **mental** and **cognitive** symptoms of anxiety include things like;

- Too much thinking about the future
- Association of the present with the future
- Less or no sleep anticipating the danger
- Mental discomfort
- Moving from one place to another without realizing where you're going
- Confusion
- Frightening dreams
- Forgetting of oneself
- Asking yes but "what if..."
- Getting obsessed

- Poor perception
- Irrational thinking.

2. Emotional, Physical and Behavioral Symptoms

The **emotional**, **physical** and **behavioral** symptoms of anxiety may include things like;

- Feelings uncomfortable
- Sad or unhappy feelings
- Sweating
- Frequent urination
- Body frightening
- Lack of confidence
- Feeling like vomiting or nausea
- In some cases, one might get diarrhea
- Shaking
- Feeling weak
- Some start stammering when trying to converse
- Rise in temperature
- Increase in heartbeat
- Dry Mouth
- Blushing
- Fainting
- Compulsion
- Continuous and repetition of work e.g. repetition of

hard washing

- Doing again and again the same thing
- Crying (in children)
- And many more.

DIAGNOSES AND PREVENTION

Psychologists and Psychiatrists can Diagnose Anxiety and phobias through;

- ❖ Diagnostic and Statistical Manual (DSM IV)
- ❖ Questionnaires and inventories e.g.
  - Zung Self Rating Anxiety Scale
  - Hamilton Anxiety Scale
  - Beck Anxiety Inventory
  - Generalized Anxiety Disorder Scale
  - Social Phobia Inventory etc.
- ❖ Psychological Tests
- ❖ Observations
- ❖ Clinical Interviews
- ❖ Case study
- ❖ And many more.

The prevention of anxiety and phobias can be done by;

- ➢ Earlier identification
- ➢ Immunization
- ➢ Avoiding alcohol especially when pregnant etc.

CHAPTER 5

17 NATURAL REMEDIES AND PSYCHOTHERAPIES TO ANXIETY

CHAPTER SUMMARY

Are you anxious?

17 effective natural remedies to relieve all humans from anxiety

ARE YOU ANXIOUS?

As a psychologist and researcher, I know that many people are anxious every day. And this was the main reason to write this book in order to see if I can make a difference in someone's life this moment am alive. We are created for the benefit of other people. This limited time God has blessed us with we can change the world positively in one way or another. I always say that I write books, young as I am now in 20's by this year 2015, enthusiastic to make a change in some one's life. And even when I will be no more, and no more time to write my already written work can be speaking on behalf of me in form of a book like this.

17 EFFECTIVE NATURAL REMEDIES TO RELIEVE ALL HUMANS FROM ANXIETY

1. Always be positive

Trying to be positive here means, trying to challenge negative thinking about the present or future. For example, if you are waiting anxiously for exam results or a clinical test results you may ask yourself this question, "Even if I get worried about the results, would I change the results?" The fact is that the results cannot change. If is in the case of exam anxiety, you cannot 'fail' if your results were 'pass.' Or in case of a clinical or medical result, you cannot become 'positive' if the results are 'negative.' The results would be as they should. Be calm always and try to be positive in all things.

2. Think that you are Important Today

Thinking that you are the most important in this world is one of the best natural remedies to lower anxiety. As we have seen, anxiety is anticipatory towards future unpleasantness. Thinking you are important and that the future is not even yours but belong to God is also a good remedy to help you lower anxiety level. Secondly practice to think your best today but not future. You may not know about the future not even a minute after this, what would happen. Think of best of today and leave the future in the hands of God.

3. Have Sky Walk (Night Walk) Daily

Having a walk alone and trying to breathe deeply in and out can reduce both phobias and anxiety.

The best walk is usually at night. When you are slightly walking, look at the sky; the stars, moon, clouds and the beauty of heaven. The fact is that when you walk looking towards the sky, your anxious thoughts start fading away and eventually you find your thoughts blending with the sky and start enjoying that healing beauty. This eventually reduces your anticipatory poor thoughts about the future and plants happy and cheering thoughts. This remedy is practically quite effective. Try it tonight and enjoy the happiness!

4. Change your Daily Leisure

This means that is you are used to go for evening leisure in the swimming pool, you may today think of visiting your best friend. By changing your daily leisure time will motivate you to a new way of life rather than you are used to. This will also prevent you from staying in one place hence reducing anxiety.

5. Share Your Worries or anxiety with a trusted person

Ensure you visit your trusted friend sometimes and try to share with him.

Sharing seems to help a lot. The more you feel like being worried or anxious the more you need to think of going to someone for a company.

6. Just Relax and have some fun

Relaxing means you should not think too much about the issue. Sit down and relax. You may wish to tension different parts of your body and relaxing them. Tension tightly for about 5 seconds and relax. Then try to have fun. Having fun means you can think of making a joke with someone or thinking of going to the beach with your loved one. Please note that the fun should not lead you to immoral acts like taking drugs, smoking, drinking or casual sex. Always know the limit for your fun.

7. Take a long cold bath (Tank full of water)

Water does a lot to relieve one from anxiety. This is what I termed as **'psycho-hydrotherapy'**. Take a long bath especially with cold water. Immerse yourself into water tank or any bathing equipment which you can use to fill enough water. As much as it may depend on you, spend more time in the water. As I have also mentioned in my book on remedies, *"63 Natural Remedies to Stress and Depression with A-Z of Happiness"* water is **'psychophilos'** meaning that you cannot separate the brain from water. They are always strong and loving friends. Psychophilos is a word from 'Psyche' which is mind and 'Philos' which is a love.

8. Drink more warm water

Not only spending much time in cold fresh water (external) but drink more water especially warm in nature. It is also a good psychophilos for anxiety and phobias. Water is the source of life and drinking a lot of it can flash off your pain and postpone your worry. Drink a lot of it as it is the natural medicine for any medical or psychological problem.

9. Get a Foot Massage

Massaging can also do better especially on the feet as feet have reflexes or have nerves which are direct to the brain. Take some quality time for massaging your feet. This can be so helpful and more effective if you combine it with remedy 6.

10. Listen to a Nice Cooling Music Daily

Music, especially religious songs which are played softly do a lot in natural treatment of anxiety. Please be sure to select wisely the songs to play because some songs are related to worries by themselves. Also please remember to play your music softly especially a spiritual song. Spiritual songs are spirit builders in nature. Listen to a song which **motivates** you.

11. Get enough Rest

Anxiety or fear causes some people not to have enough sleep. Ensure you go to your bed the same time you are used to. Have enough sleep. Sleep helps a lot in relaxing your mind. The more you sleep, the more the mind relaxes but also be careful not to oversleep. Have at least 8 hours of sleep daily.

12. Spend time with others

Spend time with positive people who influence your life positively. When you spend time with those people you will feel as if they are also sharing in your anxiety. Please be careful of the people you spend time with. Some might be more worry or anxiety contributors than your current anxiety. Be selective especially in times like this.

13. Go for an exercise in the field

Exercise is one of the effective remedies to both anxiety and phobias. Exercise regularly and do it even more especially when depressed. Aerobic exercise is so effective especially at this time you are anxious or fearing. This is because your brain requires about 20% of oxygen inhaled to help it carry out its many activities. You, therefore, need to feed it with enough oxygen especially a time like this. If you love gym, it might be good. Also walking around your garden or outside your house quietly may help a lot and is quite helpful.

14. Adopt Healthy Eating Lifestyle

Some people when anxious do not eat enough or never eat at all just depression patients. It is important you eat as usual. Start with the breakfast. Eat enough breakfast, full of legumes, vegetable, nuts and collection of fruits. Eat enough like a big manager as if you are in the Garden of Eden. Please avoid at all coffee, tea, alcohol, beer, wine, sugar and any other caffeine related substances. These do a lot of harm to your body and may also affect your sleep. Avoid alcohol, even though is rarely.

15. Visit a Clinical Psychologist, Psychiatrist or medical doctor

If you keep on having anxiety or phobia or nothing you find changing in your life even though after trying these remedies, as soon as possible consult an anxiety health professional for a consultation or for higher medication.

The earlier the better to avoid many negative symptoms which may deteriorate your health.

16. Have a 'Nature Challenge'

Try and visit natural places like rivers, lakes, mountains, trees, try to imagine being part of the nature, by participating with what that nature does. For example, if you visit a park, try to compare yourself with the birds of the air. Try and ask yourself this question, "I am created in God's image and likeness, then why should I worry when these birds don't even worry anything about their future, I should be happier than they are! Right?" This question is called **'nature challenge'** because it will definitely challenge your anxiety and find yourself happy and smiling with the nature. In other words, the nature will challenge you until you find yourself happier than itself.

The greatest mystery about nature is that it is second to God and hence I include it next to my 17th remedy 'God.' Some people say cleanness is second to Godliness but I say Nature is second to Godliness because the creation comes next after the Creator. The Creator creates and hence what he creates is second to Him. Hence nature which also includes cleanness and which is creation is second to Godliness and it shows His nature. That means nature shows the **nature of God** and second to Him. Nature assures you that you are part of it and if you are part of the nature, you are second to God. And this assures you that you are important to God. This is the basic remedy I use to improve my mental health and having deep breath always.

17. Take It to God

When anxious, just like in depression, so many negative thoughts may come along the way in your mind, like you are not important and no one loves you, and others which may lead to self-hatred about your past, present or future. But as I have mentioned in my 16th remedy to anxiety, just remember who created you? God. The ultimate Being who understands what you go through and feel. He has promised to never leave you alone nor forsake you; Deuteronomy 31:6 (text from the bible) "Be strong and courageous. **Do not be afraid** or terrified because of them, for the Lord your God goes with you; He will never leave you nor forsake you." Please read the whole verse carefully. What a beautiful and assuring God's promise. He is our God and He will never leave us. Matthew 6:25 and 31-34, (text from the bible) 25 "Therefore I tell you, **do not worry** about your life, what you will eat or drink; or about your body, what you will wear. Is not life more than food, and the body more than clothes?

31 So do not worry, saying, 'What shall we eat?' or 'What shall we drink?' or 'What shall we wear?' 32 For the pagans run after all these things and **your heavenly Father knows that you need them.** 33 But seek first his kingdom and his righteousness, and all these things will be given to you as well. 34 Therefore do not worry about tomorrow, for tomorrow will worry about itself. Each day has enough trouble of its own."

So, the most ultimate natural remedy to anxiety is trusting and doing the will of God and He has promised to care for our worries. Trust and obey Him. (For those who do not know about this God and would love to know Him, you can visit any Christian church or contact me through my personal email: **sharegodslove.withhischildren@gmail.com**).

CHAPTER 6

SLEEP, DREAMS AND SLEEP DISTURBANCES

CHAPTER SUMMARY

What Is Sleep?

Importance of Sleep

Types Of Sleep

Non-REM and REM Sleep

Stages of Sleep

Sleep Cycles

Dreams
  What Is a Dream?
  The secret behind Dreams
  Length of a Dream

How Much Sleep should a Human need?

Sleep Disturbances and Disorders

WHAT IS SLEEP?

I feel it's important we ask ourselves this question before we continue. What is really a good definition of sleep? Sleep is both psychological and physical condition in living organisms and is characterized by unconsciousness of mind, low level of brain low waves, REM or Non-REM. Also, during this time of sleep muscles seem not to react to the external environment.

Sleep normally take place during the night but in very hot climates some people find themselves sleeping during the day time.

For example, if you may visit a Muslim community especially during July month, you may find them sleeping at day time.

The time for sleep varies from place to place. Depending with the weather condition sleep may be affected in many organisms. Like in summer time, especially where the temperatures grow so high in the day, some people find it so difficult to sleep the usual time, some find themselves having difficulties in sleep. Now, let's try to see how important sleep is.

IMPORTANCE OF SLEEP

Sleep and rest are very important in every human being. So many people in life don't sleep enough. Let us now see how important sleep is to every living organism and there after we look at the amount of time needed for human being. We will look at the most important functions of sleep in the body and mind.

1. Processing and Consolidation of memory

All the learned information at day time gets processed during sleep. Amygdala part of brain is not only involved in emotions especially aggressiveness, but it is quite active during sleep in the processing of memories. In other words when one doesn't sleep enough at night, he/she might find himself/herself performing poor in class. Sleep is so crucial in memory processing and consolidation. **Consolidation** here refers to a process in which memory is stored in long term form or LTM (Long Term memory). Those who sleep enough find themselves good at remembering things easily and in examinations perform quite better.

2. Immunity Boosting

During sleep the immune system is boosted. More white blood cells are generated or formed and hence strengthens the immune system of a person. This helps keeping one free from diseases.

On contrary, sleep deprivation affects immune system. When we sleep, we prevent ourselves from many dangers associated with our immune system. When we sleep enough, we allow our immunity even fight against cancer cells.

3. Brain Development

During sleep is when the brain is thought to develop. And this is the reason why small children especially from birth (infants) sleep more than adults and they are recommended to sleep enough more than adults.

4. Energy and Security

When we sleep, we allow the body to be more energized and active the next day and hence keep us safe from dangers associated with day sleeping like car accidents. Hence, the enough time we sleep in a night the safer we become the next day.

TYPES OF SLEEP

NON-REM AND REM SLEEP

Non-REM (NREM) is a type of sleep where no rapid eye movements take place. **REM** sleep refers to Rapid Eye Movements. It is a type of sleep which involves movements of eyes rapidly, a time when dreams are thought to take place.

STAGES OF SLEEP

Non-REM stage 1

This stage occurs just between sleep and wakefulness. The muscles are active but the eyes might be found rolling slowly. At the same time, one may be opening the eyes and also closing just moderately.

Non-REM stage 2

This is the second stage of sleep. It occurs during Non-REM sleep. Theta activity is seen and sleepers find hard to wake up. At the same time the alpha waves of the stage 1 are interrupted sleep spindles and K-complexes.

Non-REM stage 3

This is now the third stage which formerly was divided into stages 3 and 4. The stage is also referred to as slow-wave sleep (SWS). It is started in the preoptic area and also it includes delta activity and high amplitude waves of less than 3.5 Hz.

Also, at this stage the sleeper is found to be less responsive to the environment.

REM

This is called Rapid Eye Movement because at this moment the sleeper's eyes are seen rapidly moving.

REM is thought to be initiated by a neurotransmitter called Acetylcholine. It is inhibited by Serotonin a neurotransmitter.

It is during REM that dreams take place. The EEG waves are seen similar to wakefulness. The oxygen consumption is also very high.

SLEEP CYCLES

Sleep goes in cycles. It proceeds in cycles of Non-REM and REM. Usually there are about 4 to 5 of the cycles per every night. The first cycle may take about the first 90 minutes of sleep and follows the following format;

NREM 1 $\rightarrow$ NREM2 $\rightarrow$ NREM3 $\rightarrow$ NREM2 $\rightarrow$ REM.

The second cycle begins and follows the same format. It thought to take more time than the first cycle spending about 100-120 minutes. All other cycles also follow the same format with more time than the proceeding cycle. All these cycles are very significant for a complete health of a person.

DREAMS

What Is a Dream?

Now as we have seen, dreams take place during REM sleep. Dreams always take place when our pleasures and wishes are not met. For example, if one dreams of being very rich it means he wishes to be rich someday.

Now another thing about dreams is that, they take place connecting someone's memories with the previous memories while sleeping. For example, if one is having a sexual dream, this is a connection with the previous memories and experiences. It means that she was in one or sometime thinking about sex, or was watching a romantic comedy where while she was watching she was having her sexual wishes like wishing she would have that actor or liking that actor. These memories are usually between the time the person slept and any other time in the past.

The secret behind Dreams

One secret about dreams is that, no matter how frightening it or they would be, they connect and remind us of our past memories stored in our minds. In other words, any dream you find having during sleep, regardless of how strange it would be, it has a close connection with your past experiences stored in your long-term memory.

Another very important thing I want you understand is that, **dreams don't tell us how our future would be, but they tell us how we wish to be in the future.**

101

According to my recent researches which I have conducted on women, more than 80% of women especially unmarried may experience sexual dreams when they think about it. The watch of pornography also has led to increase in sexual dreams by unmarried girls. Actually, in the results, there was a very close relationship between girls' dreams and the movies they used to watch.

According to Sigmund Freud, dreams are as a result of unmet **behavioral pleasures.** For example, if a girl watches pornography, she will feel in need of sex and if it is unmet immediately, the following night she may experience sexual dreams as an alert that sexual pleasure enhanced by the previous porn movie is not yet met. All pleasure in the Id must be rewarded by the Ego. If any pleasure is unmet or rewarded by the ego, the dreams arise to show that those pleasures are not yet met.

Hence as I mentioned earlier, pornography and Medias related to sex are causing a lot of negatives to the young people especially psychologically. The most important thing is to be selective in what you watch or do not watch at all if programs in the Medias are erotic or sexually misguiding.

The horror movies are another area causing people to have very terrible dreams. These horror dreams are related to horror movies just as sexual dreams are related to sexually related materials.

Length of a Dream

Some dreams take a few seconds and others may even last for minutes like 10 to 30 minutes. Usually sometime it depends on which condition the sleeper is. If her sleep is not interrupted, she can keep on having that image experience.

Another thing is people are highly and more likely to remember that dream if they are awakened during the Rapid Eye Movement (REM) phase. A normal average person might have several dreams like 3 and even 4 or 5 in one night. Each dream may occur in every sleep cycle. The first dream in the preceding cycles of 90 minute are shorter than the next dream in the next cycle of 100-120 minutes. And the third longer than

103

the second and the order in length increases as the night continues.

HOW MUCH SLEEP SHOULD A HUMAN NEED?

The amount of sleep everyone needs vary from person to person, age group to age group. The table below or next page shows general recommendations for sleep for different age groups.

Age Group	Recommended Amount of Sleep
Newborns And Infants	At least 16 to 18 hours a day
Pre-schooling age Children	At least 11 to 12 hours a day
Schooling aged children	At least 10 hours a day
Adolescents or Teens	At least 9 to 10 hours a day
All Adults and Elderly	At least 8 to 9 hours a day

SLEEP DISTURBANCES AND DISORDERS

Though we may wish to sleep enough, sometimes or most of times we might end up experiencing difficulties getting sleep or sleeping. Many people in nowadays are experiencing sleep problems because of many reasons like;

- Interrupted Circadian rhythm or not having regular or scheduled time for sleeping
- Change of temperature e.g. too hot in summer
- Eating late closer to the sleep time. This is one of the main causes of many dreams taking place. Avoiding eating late night close to sleep time can be a good remedy to have a good sleep and avoiding dreams
- Diseases and pain
- Eating too much before sleep
- Stress, Depression, anxiety and guilt
- Having or experiencing one or more sleep disorders like;
  - Insomnias
  - Parasomnias
  - Nightmares
  - Sleep terror disorder
  - Sleepwalking disorder
  - REM sleep behavior disorder
  - Apnea
  - Etc.

CHAPTER 7

13 NATURAL REMEDIES AND PSYCHOTHERAPIES TO SLEEP LOSS AND SLEEP DISTURBANCES

CHAPTER SUMMARY

Finding Problem to Sleep?

13 Most Effective Natural Remedies to Sleep Loss, Dreams, and Sleep Disturbances and Disorders

FINDING PROBLEM TO SLEEP?

It is of course that many people are having problems of sleep every day. As we have seen earlier, this could be as a result of;

- Sleep disorders
- Anxiety
- Depression
- Stress
- Guilt
- Diseases
- Pain
- And many more.

 But we can use the following remedies to help ourselves to cope up, manage or free from sleep loss. Let's see what we can do to try to improve our sleep. These remedies are quite effective and following them so carefully can do a lot in improving our sleep.

Though they may not seem effective immediately, they can emerge to be so powerful in the future.

They are natural remedies because they are based on nature as we have seen earlier in this book about natural remedies.

They can be used by all people of all ages regardless of gender.

13 MOST EFFECTIVE NATURAL REMEDIES TO SLEEP LOSS, DREAMS, AND SLEEP DISTURBANCES AND DISORDERS

1. Fix a time table for your daily sleep

The first thing you need to do is to make a timetable for your sleep. For example, you may fix it at 9 or 10 pm. This is meant to start preparing your brain to adjust to new time. The biological clock will also get adjusted with the change with physical clock.

2. Be fixed to your sleep timetable and control the eyeballs from movements (Eyeball Control)

Now the second thing you need to do is to be strict on the time scheduled. Before the scheduled time arrives, you need to keep off all sleep disturbing equipment away from your room. This includes your;

- TV
- Computer
- Phone
- Games
- Internet server
- Etc.

Keep all of them off before the fixed sleep time. This will help you to avoid the temptation which eventually leads many to prolonging in night work and busy schedules which are not really crucial in life. Keeping these away will help in avoiding the temptations and preparing you to get into operation of your sleep schedule.

When you go to bed and close your eyes, ensure the eyelid fully covers the eye. Then control **the eyeball from movements**. Eyeball is the spherical or round shaped part of your eye. It is covered by the sclera and cornea. It is mobile and keeps on moving especially when awake. For example, if you want to look to the left, the eyeball moves to the left.

111

What I mean in this remedy is that the eyes have muscles which control the eye movements. During **NREM sleep** (refer NREM sleep in the previous chapter) the eyeball (on both eyes) is not in movement. When in REM sleep (refer REM sleep in the previous chapter) the eyes are in rapid moment and at this time sleep is disturbed by dreams as someone is asleep but the brain is working controlling the involuntary movements of the eyes.

Therefore, in this remedy, be fixed to your sleep timetable first. If it's 9:00 pm, say its 9:00 pm. Get to bed. When you go to bed, **close your eyes.** Normally some people start imagining when close the eyes and some imaginations must be of exciting the brain to be aroused hence sleep is disturbed. To control, these imaginations, **try and CONTROL the eye movements.** Let the eye ball not move but be **fixed in one place.** If you control the eye ball in one place, since you are doing it voluntarily (voluntary means you are doing it manually not automatically) you give the brain some help as it controls involuntary movements of the eyes. In other words, you give rest to the brain allowing it work on controlling your sleep.

Being fixed in one place, within 5-10 minutes you will not realize that you are already asleep.

This remedy I call it **Strict Eyeball Control Technique (SECT) remedy** as it involves strictly observing your sleep time table, and secondly controlling eyeball movements to induce sleep. This **is my most effective natural remedy** I use to sleep especially in summer when weather changes dramatically. No sleeping pills required, no artificial medicine, but sleep just comes slowly and naturally. It can be so effective for all types of sleep disturbances.

3. Avoid Stimulants

Another thing is to avoid anything you may consume and causes your brain to be aroused or to be very active during sleep. These are brain stimulants chemicals. They may include;

- Coffee
- Tea
- Alcohol
- Tobacco
- Marijuana

- Cocaine
- Etc.

4. Eat your meal at least 3 hours before bed

By eating at least 3 hours before your scheduled time to sleep, will allow your brain to be little active during sleep. The sleep is controlled by **hypothalamus** and even **medulla oblongata** among many other crucial parts of the brain. Hypothalamus controls the inner biological clock as well as eating and drinking. When you eat like 10 minutes before bed, you force your brain to be very active during sleep which in most cases leads to dreams and sleep loss. Ensure you eat your meal at least 3 hours before bed to have a better sleep.

5. Eat light meals

Eating light meals like fruits salad or fruits juice at least 3 hours before bed will lead to a faster digestion just before sleep scheduled time. This will, therefore, lead to a less or no digestion during your sleep leading to a better sleep. Eat light meal and you will enjoy sleep.

6. Do not drink too much before bed

It is very important that you drink enough water or fruit juice so as to keep you away from waking at night to quench your thirst. But, ensure not to drink close to sleep or too much lest it will also lead to waking up for short calls, hence disrupting your sleep.

7. Ensure to have an evening walk just before sleep.

Evening walk just before sleep will allow your muscle to be tired and wanting to rest. In most cases people sleep deeply when they are tired than when they are not, hence, an evening walk or a short exercise before sleep time can help much.

8. Avoid Stress, Depression, Guilt and anxiety

As far as possible, try to avoid sleep disturbing related disorders like stress, depression, guilt and anxiety. This can be done by spending your time with the best people in your life. Tightening and relaxing each part of your body and meditation can be so nice to avoid stress, depression, guilt and anxiety which disrupt sleep.

9. Take a long cold bath just before Sleep (Fill the bathroom tank with water)

Just as in anxiety, water does a lot in relation to relaxation of mind. This is what I termed as **'psycho-hydrotherapy'**. Taking a long bath especially with cold water will make your mind to relax anticipating sleep. Brain also requires a cool environment in order to allow sleep.

Note that in cases of winter time, you may prefer to take bath with warm or cold water depending with your comfort. As much as it may depend on you, spend enough time in the water. As I have mentioned in some of my books in the stress remedies, water is **'psychophilos'** meaning that you cannot separate the brain from water. They are always strong and loving friends.

Also ensure your house room temperature is under control especially during summer time. Ensure that your sleeping room is well supplied with enough and fresh oxygen throughout the day. Open the widows, curtains, doors of the house especially your bed room to allow enough supply of oxygen to your bed room.

Oxygen is so important for your brain. Brain itself requires about 20% of all oxygen inhaled. It is so important that you sleep also in a room fully supplied with fresh oxygen.

This is what I call **Psycho oxygenation**. I.e. ensuring your brain is 24 hours supplied with oxygen.

10. Drink enough water at day time

Also ensure to take enough water during the day. You may need at least 2 liters of water during winter and 3 or even more during summer time depending on what you are doing to lose water from the body.

Water is good psychophilos to prepare you for sleep the following night. Water is the source of life and drinking a lot of it can flash off your pain and postpone your worries which might be disturbing your sleep. Drink a lot of it as it is the natural medicine for any medical or psychological problem.

11. Adopt a Healthy Eating Lifestyle

Good and proper diet from the morning till the whole day is a good anticipatory of a good sleep the following night. Ensure to eat good food with enough energy. Start with a special breakfast. Eat enough breakfast, full of legumes, vegetable, nuts and collection of fruits. Eat enough like a big steward as if you are in a king's garden. It is better to change your lifestyle to a vegetarian lifestyle. Drinking enough fresh fruits and vegetable juices at day time can also help in sleep.

12. Visit a Clinical Psychologist, Psychiatrist or medical doctor

If you keep having sleep failures or nothing you find changing in your sleep, as soon as possible consult a sleep health professional for a consultation or for higher medication. The earlier you do this the better so as to avoid many negative symptoms which may deteriorate your health.

13. Read the Word of God before Bed and Trust in Him

Just as I have put this remedy last, trusting in God is the ultimate **enhancement to sleep**. He is the Alpha and Omega, the Beginning and the End. The word of God has power to make you sleep well and so safely, Psalm 4:8 (text from the bible) "In peace I will lie down and sleep, for you alone, LORD, make me dwell in safety. **"Trusting in God and doing what is right, forgiving people and being closer to Him"** is the best remedy to sleep.

CHAPTER 8

SADNESS AND ACHIEVING HAPPINESS

CHAPTER SUMMARY

Sadness

Causes and Sources of sadness in life

Created to Carry each other's burdens

20 Natural Remedies for Conquering Sadness and Achieving Happiness in Your Life

SADNESS

Sadness can be defined as a state of mind when no positive arousal is around. Positive arousal means things which impress the mind leading to good feeling like happiness. Simply, sadness is opposite of happiness.

Where there is no happiness then there is no positive arousal to the brain, mind or body.

CAUSES AND SOURCES OF SADNESS IN LIFE

Sadness can be as a result of some of the previous problems we have seen like:

- Disorders
- Sleep disturbances
- Sleep loss
- Anxiety
- Depression
- Stress
- Guilt
- Diseases
- Pain

- Break up in relationships
- Separation in marriage
- Divorce
- Death of a loved one
- Social isolation
- Failures
- Poverty
- Discrimination
- Lack of jobs
- And many more.

CREATED TO CARRY EACH OTHER'S BURDENS

As a Theologian, Psychologist and Researcher I know that many people are going through many **tragedies and sadness** in life every day. And as I have said it earlier, this was the main reason to write this book in order to see if I can make a difference in someone's life this moment am alive.

You know one thing I wish to share with my readers who are reading my books is that, it is not easy to write a book. Is it? Pressing a computer key, one after the other to make a word, and another word to make a sentence, and another sentence to make a paragraph, and another paragraph to make a page, and another page to make a chapter, and another chapter to make a book, plus edit that book for errors and grammar isn't an easy thing. Let me be very sincere I don't write these books primarily to be rich. My primary purpose of doing research and pressing these computer keys is because I consider that YOU ARE IMPORTANT THAN I AM. You and other people come first in my life.

We are created for the benefit of other people as I keep on saying. This limited time God has blessed us with we can change someone's life, change the world positively in one way or another. I always say that I write books, young as I am now in 20's by this year 2015, enthusiastic to make a change in some one's life. And even when I will be no more, and no more time to write, my already written work can be speaking on behalf of me to encourage and instruct someone in form of a book like this.

We can, therefore, use the following remedies to help ourselves to cope up, manage or free from sadness. Let's see what we can do to try to conquer sadness and welcome happiness. These remedies are quite effective and following them so carefully can do a lot in conquering sadness, improving our lives and welcome happiness daily in life.

20 NATURAL REMEDIES FOR CONQUERING SADNESS AND ACHIEVING HAPPINESS IN YOUR LIFE

1. Always Strife for Positivity

Know always that life is always ups and downs. Today you may face a problem but that problem is not there to stay. Be calm always and try to be positive in all things. Avoid negative thoughts by spending time with the word of God.

2. Avoid Suicidal Thinking

In cases where you may feel life is really threatening, try to stay close and be connected to God and good friends. This will help you avoid suicidal thinking. Try always not to stay alone. Always think of mixing with others. This will help you challenge the poor thoughts.

3. Change your Daily Leisure at least once in a week

This means that if you are used to have your dinner at home every day, you may once in a week visit your best friend and have dinner with him/her. By changing your daily leisure time will motivate you to a new way of life rather than you are used to. This will also prevent you from staying in one place and makes you to be more interactive and happier in life.

4. Have Sky Walk (Night Walk) Every day

Have a night walk which I termed as sky walk daily. Having a walk alone and trying to breathe deeply in and out can boost your body pleasure higher than normal and help to reduce work tension that you had during the day.

The best walk is usually at night but if you get time in the morning can also help your body achieve pleasure and happiness. When you are slightly walking at night, always walk looking at the sky; the stars, moon, clouds and the beauty of heaven and trying to imagine being in that beauty you see above. This helps much to connect you with the sky nature and beauty boosting your happiness to a higher level. Usually, it is more pleasurable if you do it with your wife, husband or a close friend. But be careful and ensure there are no obstacles on the ground ahead of you otherwise you may fall down.

5. Take a long cold bath at least twice in a day

Ensure in the morning and evening you take bath just when you wake up and before sleeping respectively. As I said earlier, water does a lot to relieve one from many tensions. This is what I termed as **'psycho-hydrotherapy'**. Take a long bath especially with cold water. As much as it may depend on you**, spend more time in the water**. As I mentioned in my stress remedies book, water is **'psychophilos'** meaning that you cannot separate the brain from water. They are always strong and loving friends. Cold water is better but if it is in the winter, you may use warm water. This will always keep you away from many tensions and boosts your happiness daily.

6. Drink more warm water

Just as in the case of anxiety, sleep loss and also stress drink more water especially warm in nature. It is also a good psychophilos for reducing tensions and boosting your happiness. Warm water is quite nice especially when it's cold. You may prefer cool water during summer and high temperature periods or seasons. The more you drink a lot of water, the more you are sure to fight against sadness and hence promoting happiness.

7. Listen to a Nice Cooling Music Daily

Listen to a cool and spirit building music daily especially when you wake up and before you go to bed. The best are religious songs which are played softly and can do a lot in relieving you from tensions and help boosting your happiness. Please play your music softly especially a spiritual song. Spiritual songs are spirit builders in nature.

NB: Always be sure to choose the songs to play very carefully. Some songs promote sadness in nature. For example, assume you feel sad because of a broken relationship. In this case listening to a love or romantic song may promote or increase your sadness as it will remind you of the incidence. The right song to play at this time is spirit builder like a gospel song which is meant to promote encouragement.

8. Get enough Rest Daily

Sleep enough daily. (Please see the required time to sleep as per your age in chapter 6 of this book). Ensure you go to your bed the same time you are used to. Have enough sleep. Sleep helps a lot in relaxing your mind. The more you sleep the more the mind relaxes. Remember to be careful also not to oversleep. Having at least 8 hours of sleep daily if you are an adult or old age, will ensure your body is always energized boosting your happiness every day.

Having enough sleep help your body to generate energy which will make you to wake up the next day joyful, happy and cheerful ready to face the day ahead and helps to keep your mood level high. Wherever you go, you have to tell yourself or someone this acronym I form, "SIH" i.e. 'Sleep Is Happiness.' I.e. it is anti-sadness.

9. Spend time with others daily and create something new

Spend time with positive people who influence your life positively and who make you feel important and special. When you spend time with those people you will feel as if they are also part of your life especially when in pain. If you want to be happy in life spend more time with these people.

But also remember you also need time to create your new works and any other activities. As you spend more time with others you also should have your personal limits. Set amount of time to spend with your good friends. Be strict on that. Do not exceed the set time. Spending more time with others than the time you should be creating something new is not wise enough. Though you need to be happy with friends, you need of time **to create something new.**

When you create something new, which even others haven't created increases your happiness even more than the happiness from your friends. Always remember to set enough time for yourself.

When you see or remember something great you have done or accomplished, triggers your brain/mind with positive arousal which is happiness.

10. Go for an exercise in the field daily

Before the sky walk at night, its better you have an exercise day time for some time. Exercise regularly and if you love gym, it might be good. Also walking around your garden or outside your house quietly may help a lot in boosting your energy and happiness.

The exercise does much in boosting one's happiness. Not only does it promote good health, but it promotes good behavior especially which promotes happiness, reduces tension and lowers sadness.

The fact is that happiness and health go hand in hand. The more you are health, the more you are likely to be happier in life. The more you are happier in life, the more you are likely to have a better health.

11. Adopt Healthy Eating Lifestyle

Eat a balanced diet daily. Start with the breakfast. Eat enough breakfast, full of legumes, vegetable, nuts and collection of fruits. Eat enough like a big manager as if you are in your own rich garden.

To Avoid

As I have said earlier, please avoid at all;

- Sugar
- Alcohol
  - ➢ Beer
  - ➢ Wine
- Tea
- Coffee and
- Any other caffeine related substances.

These do a lot of harm to your body and may affect your health. Avoid alcohol, even though is rarely. Reduce or completely avoid sugar. By doing this your body will always be energized hence boosting your happiness.

The real secret behind happiness in many people and families is LIFESTYLE. The way you live, what you do every day, how you think about things, how you respond to different threats in life, your morality, what you eat, what you drink is all what determines your maximum happiness. This is the secret which I follow every day and I find myself being happier in life and avoiding many life threats hence facilitating my happiness.

12. Spend Enough Time focusing on your relationships

As I mentioned earlier in one of my books about **relationship stressors,** many people today are going through many sadness as a result of relationship barriers. Men and Women can be happier in life if they can conquer this threat. Most of people seem to be unhappy in life mainly because their relationships don't work.

After doing my research by asking women about whether they are happy in life, most of them who said they were happy said that it was because their relationship was fine while unhappy said they were facing relationship problems.

As I have mentioned earlier in my books, in the cause of prostitution and pornography, most of the women who had engaged in prostitution said that they were experiencing broken relationships like;

- Being widowed
- Broken love
- Divorced
- Infidelity from the husbands
- And many more relationship failures

which turned them to choose to revenge into commercial sex.

It is, therefore, wise enough to daily focus in your relationship and see how you can turn it to happiness. This includes spending a quality time with your family, children, husband and discussing your sexual life with your marriage partner and looking for all ways to improve your relationship.

Spend enough time with your loved one, wife or husband. Value the time you spend together discussing about life failures and drawbacks, life successes and progresses and looking in all ways to improve at least a step ahead every day.

13. Self-Meditation

Sometimes create time to meditate and think about yourself. Think about your good things and experiences in the past. Try and think of wishing to have the same or better experiences in the future.

Self-meditation or introspection helps much in appreciating the far you have come from. Thinking about;

- ✓ How you escaped an accident
- ✓ How you got healed from a dangerous disease

- ✓ How you got a wonderful husband
- ✓ How you got a wonderful wife
- ✓ How you got an amazing job
- ✓ How really God has blessed you with wonderful children or
- ✓ How He has kept you alive till present,

is one thing which can add up your joy and empower your happiness, actually so greatly.

14. Be More Hospitable and avoid Selfishness and be Self Contented

The biggest or one of biggest mystery behind the happiness is **giving**. Being kind to people as well as being hospitable gives a new special way to people turning your pain to joy or happiness. Those who find themselves giving eventually find themselves happy and joyful mysteriously. The secret of giving is that, you give properties in return people give you happiness. Never think of being selfish. Overcome evil by becoming good. Overcome sadness by becoming selfless.

135

Secondly, always **be contented** and **satisfied** with whatever little you have. If you have a small car, just be happy that you have, some people never even have a bicycle.

Learn to be satisfied with what you have. Your wife no matter how she looks like. Your husband, no matter the way he looks like. Your children, food and even shelter, the little money that you have. **Self-contentment** is another ideal and easy way to welcome happiness to your life and family.

15. Smile even if things are wrong

Smiles cover many pains. Smile but also remember if you are unhappy smiling alone is not enough. Share your feeling with someone you trust. As I mentioned in my book *"63 Natural Remedies to Stress and Depression With A-Z Of Happiness,"* and other books, in the case of stress, sharing is the best practice and remedy of throwing hurts and pains out of your mind. Smile then after sharing.

16. Self-Thinking Happiness

Say that it's not only you who is going through that painful experience. There are many more in the world going through the same pain. No human can be happy always. Sometimes some pains come but with trust in God they wither away soon.

17. Avoid Stress, Depression, Anxiety and Guilt

If you really follow all what I have included in this book from chapter one up to this chapter, you will be at a safe place and free from guilt, anxiety, sleep loss and sadness which are the causes of unhappiness to many people today.

Avoid them all by following all the natural remedies I have included in the proceeded chapter after or you can read more on stress and depression in my other books like; *"Women's Precious Fountain Of Well-being And Happiness,"* or *"63 Natural Remedies To Stress & Depression With A-Z Of Happiness."*

Then the next thing you feel like calling me and say, "Yes, Joe, it's really mystically working! Praise God for His curing nature!!" I'm happier than I have ever been in my life.

18. Do What Is Right and avoid Evil

As I have mentioned in the remedy 11 the main secret behind plenty of happiness in addition to eating and drinking lifestyle is, MORALITY. By doing what is right and even teaching others to do the same, is the additional secret behind much happiness in life.

As I mentioned earlier, "Disobedience is the root of all immorality and the immorality is the root of all pain." Always do what is right and you will avoid many sad instances in life. In the case of **guilt**, asking for forgiveness to your past sins and restarting your life new with God, as I have mentioned in the natural remedies to guilt, is one way to improving your happiness every day.

Remember to do what is right always and avoid evil and you will never suffer from guilt which brings inner pain and unhappiness.

Avoid evil and do what is right, the bible Amos 5:14 (text from the bible) "Seek good, and not evil, that ye may live; and so Jehovah, the God of hosts, will be with you, as ye say."

19. Spending Time with the Nature and deep inhaling flowers smells

Try and visit natural places like rivers, lakes, mountains, trees and try to imagine being part of the nature, by participating with what that nature does. For example, if you visit a lake or a river, try and put your legs in the water, and feel the movements. You may also visit a swimming pool and spend some time in the water. But be careful with yourself especially if you are so young or you don't know how to swim. This feeling gets sensed by your legs, hands, body and is sent to your brain through sensory nerves which covers the whole of your body, leading to ease feeling and joy in your brain and your whole body, therefore, boosting your happiness.

Another example of the nature is visiting natural flower gardens, spending **sometime deep inhaling flesh smells** from beautiful flowers. Some flowers have so nice and sweet smells. Deep inhaling these smells refreshes your mind from tensions and sadness improving happiness. As much as it may depend on you, spend much time with the flowers in the garden.

Another example of nature is going out for a tour, walking in the beach, or visiting a park and seeing the natural creations can do much as a reminder that **you are part of that nature.** Nature is friendly and even if you feel hated, when spending time with nature like animals helps one to recover naturally and feels important. The nature provides a special happiness and healing power from God of heaven and is one of the most ultimate sources of happiness power and, therefore, I put it close to the 20th, the last most effective natural remedy to conquering sadness and achieving happiness, "God."

20. Trusting in God

The Lord is the ultimate joy and happiness to all. He feels our pains, carry us to a happy breeze and we are restful.

David says in Psalms 63:5-7 (text from the bible) "My soul will be satisfied as with fat and rich food, and my mouth will praise you with joyful lips, when I remember you upon my bed, and meditate on you in the watches of the night; for you have been my help, and in the shadow of your wings I will sing for joy."

Being close to God as well as **doing what is right** is an ultimate way to be happy in life. God loves His people and is happy when we all are happy. His purpose and aim are to see us happy and even happier in this life as well as the life to come.

Trust and obey Him every day and He will surely sustain your happiness and even add more and more.

BIBLIOGRAPHY

Note: Most of the research in this book I did personally and face to face from men and women by the help of my new system in Psychology, 'Psychemoanalysis' where I had developed a HMQ test. The method I applied in doing my face-to-face research was; field survey, case study, observation, interviews, questionnaires and psychemotherapies including online. The rest of the research I compared my personal research with the bible and others researchers and psychologists.

FURTHER READINGS

Abramowitz, J. S. (2004). Treatment of obsessive-compulsive disorder in patients who have comorbid major depression. *Journal of Clinical Psychology,* 60, 1133–1141.

Allen, E. S., & Atkins, D. C. (2012). The association of divorce and extramarital sex in a representative U.S. sample. *Journal of Family Issues*, 33, 1477–1493.

Atkins, D. C., Baucom, D. H., & Jacobson, N. S. (2001). Understanding infidelity: Correlates in a national random sample. *Journal of Family Psychology*, 15, 725–749.

Bandelow, B., Baldwin, D., Abelli, M., et al (2017). Biomarkers for anxiety disorders, OCD and PTSD: a consensus statement part II. Neurochemistry, neurophysiology and neurocognition. *World J Biol Psychiatry.* 18(3):162–214.

Baumeister, R. F., Dale, K., & Sommer, K. L. (1998). Freudian defense mechanisms and empirical findings in modern social psychology: Reaction formation, projection, displacement, undoing, isolation, sublimation and denial. *Journal of Personality, 66*(6), 1081–1095.

Bible Study Tools (2014). Salem Web Networks. The Bible - (biblestudytools.com).

Bornstein, R. F. (1996). Beyond orality. *Psychoanalytic Psychology, 13*, 177–203.

Brewin, C. R, Andrews, B., Valentine, J. D. (200). Meta-analysis of risk factors for posttraumatic stress disorder in trauma-exposed adults. *Journal of Consulting and Clinical Psychology,* 68 (5), 748–766.

Bruce, M. L. & Hoff, R. A. (1994). Social and physical health risk factors for first-onset major depressive disorder in a community sample. Social Psychiatry and Psychiatric Epidemiology, 29, 165–171.

Foa, E. B. & Meadows, E. A. (1997). Psychosocial treatments for posttraumatic stress disorder: critical review. *Annu. Rev. Psychol,* 48, 449–480. [PubMed] [Google Scholar].

Mayo Clinic (2014). Major Depressive Disorder. Mayo Clinic. Depression (major depressive disorder) - Symptoms and causes - Mayo Clinic.

McLeod, S. A. (2013). Kohlberg's Stages of Moral Development. Simply Psychology. https://www.simplypsychology.org/kohlberg.htm.

O'Brien, C. (2008). Sustainable happiness: How happiness studies can contribute to a more sustainable future. *Canadian Psychology / Psychologie canadienne, 49*(4), 289–295.

Ramar K, Malhotra RK, Carden KA, et al. Sleep is essential to health: an American Academy of Sleep Medicine position statement. *J Clin Sleep Med.* 2021;17(10):2115–2119.

Rásky É., Waxenegger A., Groth S., Stolz E., Schenouda M., Berzlanovich A. (2017). Sex and gender matters: a sex-specific analysis of original articles published in the Wiener klinische Wochenschrift between 2013 and 2015. *Wiener Klinische Wochenschrift,* 129(21-22):781–785. doi: 10.1007/s00508-017-1280-1.

Tantry, T. (2019). Anxiety and depression during period: Causes, detection, and treatment. Flo.health. Retrieved January 2020 from https://flo.health/menstrual-cycle/health/anxiety-depression-during-period.

Watson, S. (2018). How to Deal with premenstrual depression. healthline. Retrieved January 2020 from https://www.healthline.com/health/pms-depression.

Classic Books for a Better Lifestyle and Excellent Future from a Life changing Author.

Order Today: From Amazon.com; John Zedgenbroth Joe.

Or Call +254725266986.

Or Email: sharegodslove.withhischildren@gmail.com

www.ingramcontent.com/pod-product-compliance
Lightning Source LLC
Chambersburg PA
CBHW070917290526
45795CB00001B/345